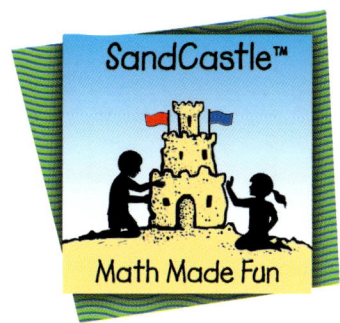

We Have the Skills to Know U.S. Bills!

Tracy Kompelien

Consulting Editors, Diane Craig, M.A./Reading Specialist
and Susan Kosel, M.A. Education

Published by ABDO Publishing Company, 4940 Viking Drive, Edina, Minnesota 55435.

Copyright © 2007 by Abdo Consulting Group, Inc. International copyrights reserved in all countries. No part of this book may be reproduced in any form without written permission from the publisher. SandCastle™ is a trademark and logo of ABDO Publishing Company.

Printed in the United States.

Credits
Edited by: Pam Price
Curriculum Coordinator: Nancy Tuminelly
Cover and Interior Design and Production: Mighty Media
Photo Credits: Photodisc, ShutterStock, Wewerka Photography

Library of Congress Cataloging-in-Publication Data

Kompelien, Tracy, 1975-
   We have the skills to know U.S. bills! / Tracy Kompelien.
     p. cm. -- (Math made fun)
   ISBN 10 1-59928-549-5 (hardcover)
   ISBN 10 1-59928-550-9 (paperback)

   ISBN 13 978-1-59928-549-8 (hardcover)
   ISBN 13 978-1-59928-550-4 (paperback)
   1. Paper money--United States--Juvenile literature. 2. Money--United States--Juvenile literature.
 3. Dollar, American--Juvenile literature. I. Title.

HG591.K66 2007
332.4'973--dc22

2006021569

SandCastle Level: Transitional

SandCastle™ books are created by a professional team of educators, reading specialists, and content developers around five essential components—phonemic awareness, phonics, vocabulary, text comprehension, and fluency—to assist young readers as they develop reading skills and strategies and increase their general knowledge. All books are written, reviewed, and leveled for guided reading, early reading intervention, and Accelerated Reader® programs for use in shared, guided, and independent reading and writing activities to support a balanced approach to literacy instruction. The SandCastle™ series has four levels that correspond to early literacy development. The levels help teachers and parents select appropriate books for young readers.

Emerging Readers
(no flags)

Beginning Readers
(1 flag)

Transitional Readers
(2 flags)

Fluent Readers
(3 flags)

These levels are meant only as a guide. All levels are subject to change.

A dollar bill
is a piece of paper money.

Words used to describe bills:
**bill
denomination
dollar
money**

three
3

These are U.S. dollar bills.

We use  to buy things.

Bills come in different amounts, or denominations.

This is a one-dollar bill.

I use a  to buy a  .

This is a five-dollar bill.

I use a  to buy a toy  .

This is a ten-dollar bill.

I use a  to

buy a  .

This is a twenty-dollar bill.

I use a  to buy a  .

This is a fifty-dollar bill.

I use a  to buy a new 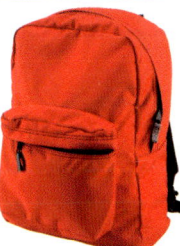 .

We Have the Skills to Know U.S. Bills!

ten
10

Ian raises money
for his school.
He loves to do it.
He thinks it's cool.

Ian sells boxes of cookies for five dollars each. Each box he sells comes with a thank-you speech.

fourteen
14

Ian sells 10 boxes in one day. He's a good salesman, what can we say?

I received 10 five-dollar bills. That is the same as $50.

Bills Every Day!

sixteen
16

Betsy and her mom pay for the movie tickets with two five-dollar **bills**.

eighteen
18

After we have a garage sale, we count how many **dollars** we have made.

twenty
20

Billy gives the lunch lady a one-dollar bill for his school lunch.

twenty-two
22